IMAGES
of America

STEVENS COUNTY

IMAGES
of *America*

STEVENS COUNTY

Stevens County Historical Society

ARCADIA
PUBLISHING

Copyright © 2007 by Stevens County Historical Society
ISBN 978-1-5316-2452-1

Published by Arcadia Publishing
Charleston SC, Chicago IL, Portsmouth NH, San Francisco CA

Library of Congress Catalog Card Number: 2006924327

For all general information contact Arcadia Publishing at:
Telephone 843-853-2070
Fax 843-853-0044
E-mail sales@arcadiapublishing.com
For customer service and orders:
Toll-Free 1-888-313-2665

Visit us on the Internet at www.arcadiapublishing.com

CONTENTS

ACKNOWLEDGMENTS

We wish to acknowledge the hard work and dedication of all the volunteers of the publications committee. Narratives that correctly identified the photographs while entertaining and educating our audience were sometimes difficult to achieve decades or a century after the photograph was taken. The choices about which photographs to include were also very difficult. Time, availability, or quality of photographs and publication space were all factors. We plan future subject-themed publications that will allow for more images of Stevens County to be showcased.

Our spring 2006 University of Minnesota, Morris interns, Erika Paulson and Kate Borman, scanned many of these photographs and typed in the information we began with. Carol Day, former director of the Stevens County Historical Society and current editor of the "Looking Back" column in the *Morris Sun-Tribune*, was good enough to attend countless meetings to help verify information or identify people, buildings, or events in the photographs. She also spent many hours writing captions. Without Carol's knowledge of Stevens County, Pearl Diers and Ardath Larson (who helped to research many of the captions) would still be looking for information.

Special thanks must go to Ardath Larson, who was responsible for making sure handwritten notes were typed into the computer to be put into this volume; LeAnn Dean helped scan in more photographs at the last minute to ensure coverage of the entire county. Tami Plank, historian/researcher, and Tina Didreckson, office specialist/genealogist for the Stevens County Historical Society, must be acknowledged as well. The part-time staff worked after-hours and weekends without pay to make this publication possible.

All of the images in this book come from the archives of the Stevens County Historical Society.

INTRODUCTION

Almost every local historical organization seeks to capture moments of the area's history on paper. The visual image has a powerful impact. The images in this publication are from the collection of the Stevens County Historical Society. From over 20,000 possible photographs, these have been chosen to represent the categories, differing demographics, and decades in the life of the county.

From a personal perspective, I am an avid photographer of the history of events and happenings in my family as well as community life. I grew up with a sense of preserving history through images. Through those family pictures one can know what great-grandma wore for everyday, what flowers she planted in her gardens, and who she invited to celebrate the special events of her life. If you believe that family photographs are valuable to your own history, then think of the importance of a collection of photographs depicting the history of a county. The photograph collection is considered one of the greatest assets a historical society has, especially when there is a description or identification with it. This book gives us an opportunity to share some of those pictorial experiences of history with others.

Images shown in this book are by no means the only images that might have been chosen. Within these pages is a sampling of photographs, snapshots taken in our county as it has grown, developed, and evolved from a land with bright blue skies, picturesque wetlands, and rolling prairies to an era in history of becoming an agricultural, educational, social, and economic center to the residents that dwell here.

The pictorial history represented is not as much about major historical events, but more about people and places and the things that occupy their time as they live out their history. Oftentimes a good picture will convey a better sense of the history of a place than a whole book of facts, figures, and dates. Looking at these photographs, really looking, will tell multitudes about the details of clothing, architecture, everyday tools, and the times in which the photograph was taken. "A picture is worth a thousand words," but only if the viewer does more than scan the image.

And so, we pass along these snapshots of our past, leaving it to the reader of the present and future to determine what they will remember and what they will pass along.

Randee L. Hokanson
Director
Stevens County Historical Society

One

AGRICULTURE

Applications to have federal land transferred to the homesteader in Stevens County were filed with several different federal land offices. The first two homestead applications were filed with the Alexandria land office in 1870. Of the 1,203 applications filed with the Federal Bureau of Land Management from 1870 to 1916, 84 were in the names of women. Peter and Anna Hanson owned a farm in Scott Township. Peter emigrated from Denmark in 1879, came to Stevens County in 1903, and erected this home in 1904.

The Hellebust Farm was located one mile west of Donnelly in Donnelly Township. Anders Olson Hellebust was a native of Norway who arrived in Donnelly in 1888. He worked at the Barrett Ranch before homesteading this land. The older part of the home was built in 1890.

Rural mail service began in Stevens County in 1903. One of the first mail carriers was Mary Kane, whose route was in Framnas and Swan Lake Townships. The picture shows her winter rig. A heated soapstone kept her feet warm. She would stop for lunch at the Carlson place in Swan Lake Township, exchange the cooler stone for one heated in the Carlson's oven, put her feet on the well-wrapped stone, and be on her way.

Frank Schott is pictured here seeding grain with a team of three horses and an ox in Stevens Township in 1920. Born in 1880, Schott was a native of Germany. He came to Stevens County at age 29. He was well known for his masonry work.

This is a steam engine from around 1910. Steam engines like as this one supplied power for plowing and threshing, revolutionizing agriculture and farmwork.

This Stevens County family poses with a Hart-Parr tractor. This kind of tractor was used to plow the prairie soil. The Hart-Parr Gasoline Engine Company was founded by Charles Walter Hart and Charles H. Parr while they attended the Iowa State College of Agriculture and Arts. Their traction engines, or tractors, were said to be the finest in the business.

This is a horse-drawn Deering Ideal grain binder from the 1920s. The paddle-wheel reel shown behind the farmer bent the wheat down toward the cutting blades. The cut straws fell on a slatted rotating canvas that moved them across to another pair of canvases. When there were enough straws gathered against this bar, the pressure made the binder mechanism work. A large curved needle threaded with twine would dart out and carry the twine over the bundle. The twine was pulled tight around the straws, a knot was tied, the twine was cut, and the needle returned to its place. The bundles rested on the carrier until the farmer pulled a lever to drop them. The bundles were gathered into shocks and left to dry before threshing.

This is a threshing crew working in the Alberta area. This threshing machine was run by steam and fueled by straw. Threshing is the process by which the seed or grain of a cereal is separated from the straw.

Meal times were always an important time for families to get together on the farm, no matter where they ate. During the time this picture was taken, farmers used every spare hour of daylight they could. Lunches (forenoon and afternoon snacks), dinners (noon), and suppers were usually eaten where and when the equipment stopped. This is Harry Day's threshing crew in 1910. The Day farm was located in section 1 of Rendsville Township. The men shown here eating lunch are Peter Falk, two unknown men, and Fred Bruns. The young boy with a doughnut and cup is Roderick Gaffney. Jess Day (Montgomery) is serving the lunch. The ladies standing are, from left to right, Margaret Wagner, Alice Kloos, and Helena Wagner, who later married Harry Day in 1917.

Stacking hay on the Tomlin farm in Darnen Township around 1910 was much easier once they got this overshot hay stacker. The sweep rake swept up the hay onto the forks of the stacker. The forks were mounted at the end of two long arms that were hinged to another frame placed vertically against the haystack. A horse-powered pulley and cable system raised the arms and forks up over the top of the stack and dumped it. The extra horse in the photograph was used to move the stacker forward as the stack built up. It was considered superior to a hay slide because it allowed much taller stacks to be built.

14

Julius Hawkinson (Hoganson), a native of Norway and a longtime resident of Hodges Township, was one of the old-time threshers. It was an exciting day when the big engine and separator was set up on the farmer's yard. The separator man, bundle haulers, "spike" pitchers, and grain haulers all had their special jobs to keep the operation running smoothly.

F. H. Richardson is seen with a corn wagon around 1920. F. H. Richardson served as pastor of the Congregational church in Morris from 1901 to 1904. During this time, he acquired a farm in Synnes Township. In 1904, he moved to Iowa but returned in 1916 to live on his farm. The family moved to Morris in 1930.

Frank Gieselman is seen here hauling grain into Chokio in 1919. Gieselman was a native of Germany who came to the United States in 1881 and to Stevens County in 1910. He farmed in Pepperton Township but later moved to Darnen Township. Gieselman also took an active part in community and public affairs.

This is the Stevens County Fair in 1912. The annual fair is one of the county's most popular institutions, and one of its oldest. The Stevens County Agriculture Society was organized in 1879 and purchased this site on the south edge of Morris in the early 1900s. The large tent on the right housed the display of the Morris Implement Company. The small tent on the left housed the display from Stone and Munro.

Here is a view of elevator row in Chokio. There were once five elevator companies in the city of Chokio. At the agricultural peak, there were 15 to 18 elevator companies in the entire county. The small town of Alberta had five at one time.

This is the Farmers' Elevator in Chokio, which was owned by S. Stewart of Morris and operated by Thomas Schmid and L. J. Flynn. The grain elevator was one of the "prairie battleships" that provided a market for the farmer's wheat and other small grain crops.

The Corn and Alfalfa Show, sponsored by the West Central Minnesota Development Association, was held on December 10–12, 1913, in Morris. The show stressed the fact that corn and alfalfa could be raised in this area and that diversified farming is better farming. Thousands of people, including 1,200 from Pope County alone, attended the show. Remarkably mild weather prevailed while it was in progress. Prominent speakers included Minnesota governor A. O. Eberhart, University of Minnesota president George Vincent, and the "Empire Builder" James J. Hill. A giant corn shock decorated the intersection of Sixth Street and Atlantic Avenue, and the Alfalfa Arch stretched across Atlantic Avenue at Seventh Street.

Atlantic Avenue in Morris was lined with automobiles during the Corn and Alfalfa Show in December 1913. The Alfalfa Arch spans Atlantic Avenue in the background.

Atlantic Avenue is seen here at night with decorations from the 1913 Corn and Alfalfa Show.

VOSS
MINN

21

Pictured here are visitors to the Stevens County Fair in 1912.

This is the newly completed Stevens County Fairgrounds grandstand that was finished just in time for the 1912 fair.

Arnold Huebner stands with his sheep around 1910. The farm family raised sheep for food and sale and used their wool for clothing.

Shown here is Hulda (Drechsler) Gausman, wife of William Henry Gausman, feeding chickens around 1910. The farm wife and children were usually responsible for feeding the chickens and gathering the eggs. Young chickens may have been eaten for Sunday dinner. When the chickens no longer laid eggs, they wound up in a soup pot and fed the family once again.

Here is a beautiful snapshot of Page Lake in Hodges Township, north of Hancock, from about 1910. Sadly by 1934, the lake was dry because of drought and the impact of county ditching programs, but it recovered to become Hancock's primary recreation area.

In the early 1900s, a group of western Stevens County citizens decided the answer to their wet fields was to dredge the land. Not all citizens agreed with this approach, but the dredging did take place beginning in 1906 after much debate. While some of the land under the lakes was farmable, other parts were not.

Two

ARTS AND CULTURE

This photograph of the Morris Social Literary Group is from 1890. This club was founded for the purpose of promoting the reading and discussion of books and literature of the day. An agenda was set and published each year. Seen here are, from left to right, (first row) Etta Cooley, Ida S. Hancock, and Flo Elmer; (second row) W. F. Cooley Sr., Lou Richardson, Grace Phelps, and F. A. Hancock.

The Mayflower Club was started in 1912 in Pepperton Township by Amanda Bach Hoyer. It later became known as the Cheerful Helpers Club. The club served as a social outlet for women and girls of the community and soon had a purpose of helping people in need in the days before welfare. After 61 years of service to the community, the club disbanded in 1973.

Although women had not yet been given the right to vote, local ladies played an active part in several civic organizations such as the Civic League, the Students Club, the Literary Club, the Red Cross, and the board of education. Pictured are, from left to right, (first row) Ida Hancock; (second row) Clara Light and an unidentified woman; (third row) Ella Spooner. These ladies were all very active in the community.

Fountain, City Park, Morris, Minn.

This Morris park has changed over the past century but is still a popular destination for families and children and is the current location for many Prairie Pioneer Days events, celebrated by county residents during the second weekend in July. The block of land, now known as East Side Park, on East Seventh Street was presented to the city by James J. Hill early in the 1900s. This site was once a slough, but by 1920 it was filled and leveled. Grass and trees were planted, and flowers and this fountain were added. The fountain has since been filled in. A bandstand was erected where concerts were presented for the public's enjoyment on summer evenings. Shown here is a fountain in East Side Park.

Morris's Carnegie Library was built in 1905 by F. A. Hancock with a $10,000 grant from Andrew Carnegie; this building housed the Morris City Library until 1970. The library became home to the Stevens County Historical Society and Museum in 1972. A 7,000-square-foot addition was added in 2005, and the building is currently listed on the National Register of Historic Places. The library is pictured here around 1920.

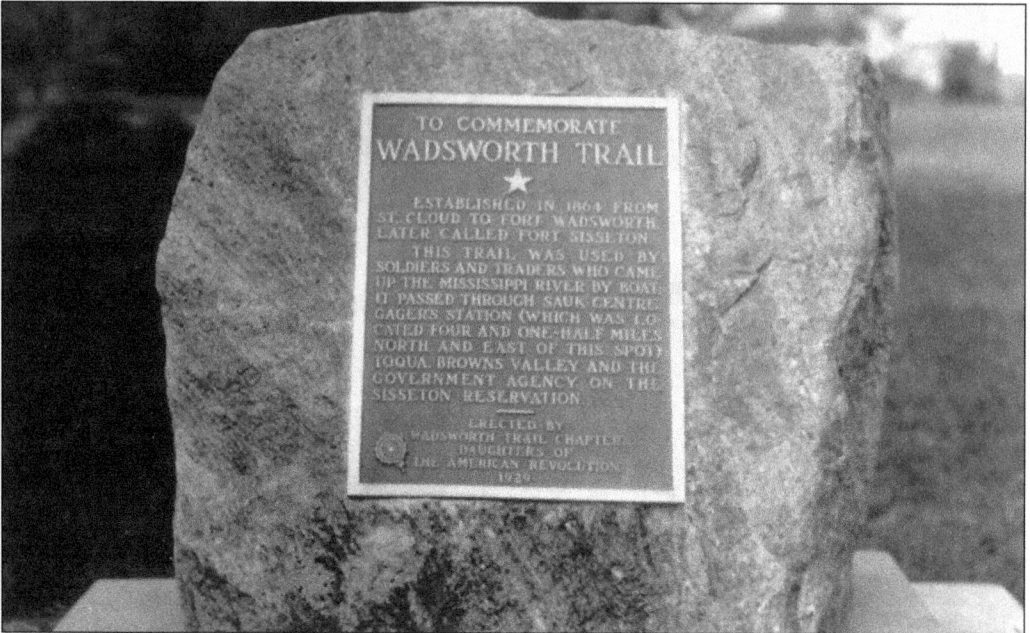

This marker was placed in the East Side Park in Morris by the Wadsworth Trail Chapter of the Daughters of the American Revolution (DAR). Trail markers were erected by members of the DAR to commemorate the brave deeds of early trailblazers. On Friday, October 4, 1929, the state regent of the DAR, Caroline E. Punderson of St. Paul, gave an address, and Grace Hall gave a historical account about the founding, use, and abandonment of the Wadsworth Trail. According to newspaper accounts of October 11, 1929, almost all the schoolchildren of the city attended, as well as many others. The event was also reported in St. Cloud and St. Paul newspapers. The marker in Morris was dedicated on October 11, 1929, in the East Side Park.

This image is of the Wadsworth Trail in 1926, 50 years after this important trade route was replaced by the railroad. A 1998 soil compaction study published in the *Soil Science Society of America* journal stated that if left unplowed, remnants may still be there in 2098.

Shown here is the Hancock Orchestra in 1892. They are, from left to right, (first row) Mabel Helgerson and H. A. Chase (conductor); (second row) K. C. Helgerson, I. T. Tollofson, and W. Muir; (third row) Kip Parks, Mr. Fisher, Frank Wilcox, Lew Wheeler, and August Erickson.

The Kongsvinger Symphonia Band, associated with Kongsvinger Free Lutheran Church of Rendsville Township, existed from about 1907 until 1924. The band produced a concert series and played for community events in the surrounding area. Originally it was directed by Rev. J. C. Abs from Hancock and later by Adolph Sherstad. Seen here are, from left to right, (first row) Albert Johnson and Peter Awsumb; (second row) Joseph Wilson, Professor Kask, Emil Awsumb, Reverend Abs, Conrad Sherstad, Adolph Sherstad, and L. P. Norby; (third row) Henry Peterson, Matt Jergenson, Alfred Wilson, Martin Jergenson, Victor Wilson, and Lawrence Brandt; (fourth row) L. O. Hanson, Ole Awsumb, Alec Hanson, Carl Anderson, and M. B. Strand.

Formed in 1896 under the direction of H. B. Lund, the Morris Cadet Band played around the area. A note attached to the back of the photograph reads "Lunds Band (originally December 1896, but this picture could have been taken later) [back row, left to right:] Lawrence Thomasson, Otto Jacobson, H. B. Lund, George Flynn(?) [middle row, left to right:] James O'Malley, Arthur Flatner, Oscar Flatner, Hilfred Thomasson [front row, left to right:] Gus Amborn(?), Ludwig Danielson, Will Haight(?), Orrin Flynn." The *Morris Tribune* of December 30, 1896, lists two (Louie Larson and Vincent Caswell) who apparently dropped out before this picture was taken. Please note that the instrumentation listed in the 1896 newspaper does not correspond to the instruments held by the players in the photograph, so the identification given above should not be taken as entirely accurate.

Pictured here are the Modern Woodmen of America, Morris Camp, No. 3184. This was one of several lodges organized for fraternal and social purposes. Insurance benefits were available through the organization. The organization appealed to middle-class men.

Anton Watzke was the director of the Morris Boy's Band. Pictured here are, from left to right, (first row) Bud Cairney, Lloyd Slawson, Johnny Hogan, Henry Watzke, Vincent Kohler, and Robert Krueger; (second row) Anton Watzke Jr., Harry Peterson, Henry Dushek, and Otto Hogan; (third row) Robert Stenger, Ed Dablow, Harold Vinje, Sylvester Eul, Edmund Hanrahan, and George Larson; (fourth row) Leo Rudnicki, Harry Nelson, Anton Watzke Sr., Othmar Treinen, William Knupple, William Sobey, and George Leuty.

Shown here is the Alberta Band around 1913. They are, from left to right, (first row) Wes Ernst, Paul Andert, Harold Buckley, Walter Bengston, Harold Gorder, Mr. Harvey (band leader), and George De Young; (second row) Pete Loften, Pete Olson, Gilbert Gulbrandson, Joe Eystad, John Eystad, Adolph Andert, Joe Weinand, and Clyde Roberts.

This is the Little German Band, also known as the Little Thirsty Four, in the 1930s. They are, from left to right, "Gob" Anderson, Bernard Olson, Hubert Grosland, and Conrad Tritten.

Pictured here is the cast of *If I Were a King* at the Assumption Church. The cast includes Rev. Edward Jones, Ann McCarthy, Joseph Eul, Ralph Hanlon, Roman Walz, Robert O'Brian, Joseph Kirwin, Henry Kirwin, Anthony Storck, Arthur Cairney, William Jaist, and Henry Schmidt.

Here is the cast of the Gilbert and Sullivan comic operetta *Pirates of Penzance* at the Orpheum Theatre. Performances took place May 7 and 8, 1915. The gypsy costume is in Stevens County Historical Society collection.

Here is the cast of the play *The Old Fashioned District School*. The play was given at the Courthouse Hall in 1895 by the Floral Club (later the Students Club) to raise funds to further interest in gardening by distributing seeds, shrubs, and the like. Seen here are, from left to right, (first row) W. P. Fowler, Mrs. J. W. Harris, Henry Leaman (or Dr. Harris?), Ida Hancock, Mrs. Charles Garlick, and Mrs. Henry Wolff; (second row) Savylla Elliot, Mrs. Brown, Mrs. Curtiss, Mrs. H. W. Stone, Mary Pearce, Mary Butterfield, and A. A. Stone; (third row) Mrs. Messersmith, Mrs. Getz, S. J. Stebbins, Charles Pepper (tall), J. D. Gillespie, F. E. Newell, H. Ward Stone, Henry Wolff (or Pete Ross?), Dr. H. L. Hulburd, Rev. A. H. Tebbets, and Mrs. Tebbets.

This is the cast of the play *Queen Esther* from around 1900.

The Strand Theater was one of two theaters in Morris owned by Joseph Gaffney. The other was the Orpheum, purchased from C. J. Muckler. The Strand Theater was built in 1916. The first movie shown there was *The Birth of a Nation*, described at the time as "the greatest film sensation ever brought to Morris". In 1923, both theaters were sold to B. J. Benfield. The first talking film in Morris was shown on March 2, 1929, after much upgrading of the technical facility in the Strand Theater.

Three

BUSINESS AND INDUSTRY

This photograph of the Kerl and Watzke blacksmith shop was taken in the late 1890s. This partnership and its 11 employees worked at a location on Sixth Street, next door to Fowler's Feed Mill, Wood Yard, and Electric Power Company on the corner of Sixth Street and Oregon Avenue. Its former location is now the parking lot between the current Ottertail Power Company building and the former Citizens Bank Building and City Center Mall.

Taken in 1900, this photograph shows J. Christiansen, who delivered milk and dairy products to village residents who did not have cows of their own. Several local businesses made deliveries to village homes using horses and wagons. Family needs were supplied by the milk wagon, grocery wagon, ice wagon, coal wagon, and the peddler's wagon. The wagons were usually painted to advertise the business making the delivery. The last horse-drawn milk wagon in Morris was used by J. J. Baer of the People's Dairy. His faithful horse, Nellie, died in 1931, and she was replaced by a shiny new truck.

Shown here is the John Conroy Well Drilling Company of Hancock about 1915 using a wooden beam well-drilling rig. The Conroy Well Drilling Company is still in operation today.

This is the interior of the Loften Brother's blacksmith shop operated by Pete and Axel Loften. The photograph was taken sometime between 1910 and 1912.

The West Central School of Agriculture wood shop class is pictured here around 1920.

The Syverson and Thorstad Tin Shop was located on East Fifth Street in Morris. Owners were Thory Syverson and Andrew Thorstad. They were advertised as "Manufacturers and Dealers in Tinware, Stoves, Sewing Machines, Iron and Wooden Pumps, Machine Oils, Paints, Etc."

The *Hancock Record* was started by Edward J. Bahe in 1899, when the type was set by hand. In addition to this weekly paper, the shop did printing jobs such as auction bills, posters, and business stationery. This is a photograph of the print shop.

The Hancock Auto Company was started in 1917 when the three Steinbring brothers, Andrew, Emil, and Henry, moved into Hancock from Darnen Township where they had engaged in farming. They sold the Mitchell, Dort, and Dodge vehicles. In 1924, they dropped the Mitchell and Dodge line and sold Chevrolets and Dorts. They also sold Hart-Parr tractors and the Avery line. A name change happened in 1926, and the business became the Steinbring Brothers Chevrolet Sales and Service. The business kept growing, changing, and improving. By 1958, Andrew's son Bob became owner. The biggest change came in 1965 when Bob moved Steinbring Chevrolet to Alexandria. The building in Hancock was in operation for several more years before it closed down.

An early photograph, from about 1910, is of the interior of the Hancock Auto Company, owned and operated by the Steinbring Brothers—A. J. (Andy), E. F. (Emil), and Henry A. (Hinny).

Charles Leamon was one of the pioneer residents of Chokio. He came to the area as a farmer but moved into town in the early 1900s and started a hardware store with his son Howard. The family sold the store later to L. C. Dorweiler. This is Leamon's Hardware Store in Chokio, pictured in about 1910.

The Grove Department Store was located on the east side of Atlantic Avenue, between Seventh and Eighth Streets. The building on the corner (hidden by the young tree) housed the First National Bank and later the Citizens Bank. Eul's Hardware took over the occupancy of the building in 1940. The third generation of the Eul family now operates the business. Grove Department Store was owned by John Grove, a leading citizen identified with the development of Morris and Stevens County. The Morris Hotel occupied the upper floors. The building burned in 1932. Aldred and Habicht Department Store was built there in 1947. The site is currently occupied by Cullen's Home Center.

Chalk's Saloon in Donnelly is pictured here around 1900.

Pictured here is the interior of the J. C. Phifer Store in Donnelly. This store burned in the Donnelly fire in 1916.

This photograph is of an unknown Stevens County dry goods and clothing store. Judging by the clothing styles, this photograph was taken between 1910 and 1915.

Linne's Bakery was located at 501 Atlantic Avenue in Morris. John Linne and his daughter Myrtle are shown with the delicacies they baked and decorated for customers. Shown here is the interior of Linne's Bakery around 1915.

Hotel William was located in block 18, lots 11 and 12 of the original town of Hancock.

Built in 1900 as the Teepee-Tonka, a hotel and business block, this hotel was renamed the La Grand Hotel in 1910. In addition to being a hotel, this site was home to an office complex, an icehouse, a public dining room, sample rooms, a marble shop, and a millinery. It was located on the northeast corner of Pacific Avenue and Seventh Street, the current site of the Stevens, Grant, Traverse Public Health building. The lot across the street that contained the sparkling fountain and green space is now home to Morris Commercial Printing.

Palm Café in Donnelly is seen in the 1920s. The owner was T. A. (Thorval) Olsen.

Here is the Scofield Restaurant in Donnelly in 1910. Pictured here are, from left to right, Bertha Scofield, Emma Olson, and Mr. and Mrs. Eugene Scofield.

The butcher, wearing the traditional white apron, is busy sharpening his knife. The Eystad building also housed a grocery store, harness shop, and pool hall on the ground floor. The Eystads and two other families lived on the top floor. John Eystad of Alberta owned the meat market shown in this photograph from around 1910. When Eystad sold out, Ted Rentz started a cream station in the same building.

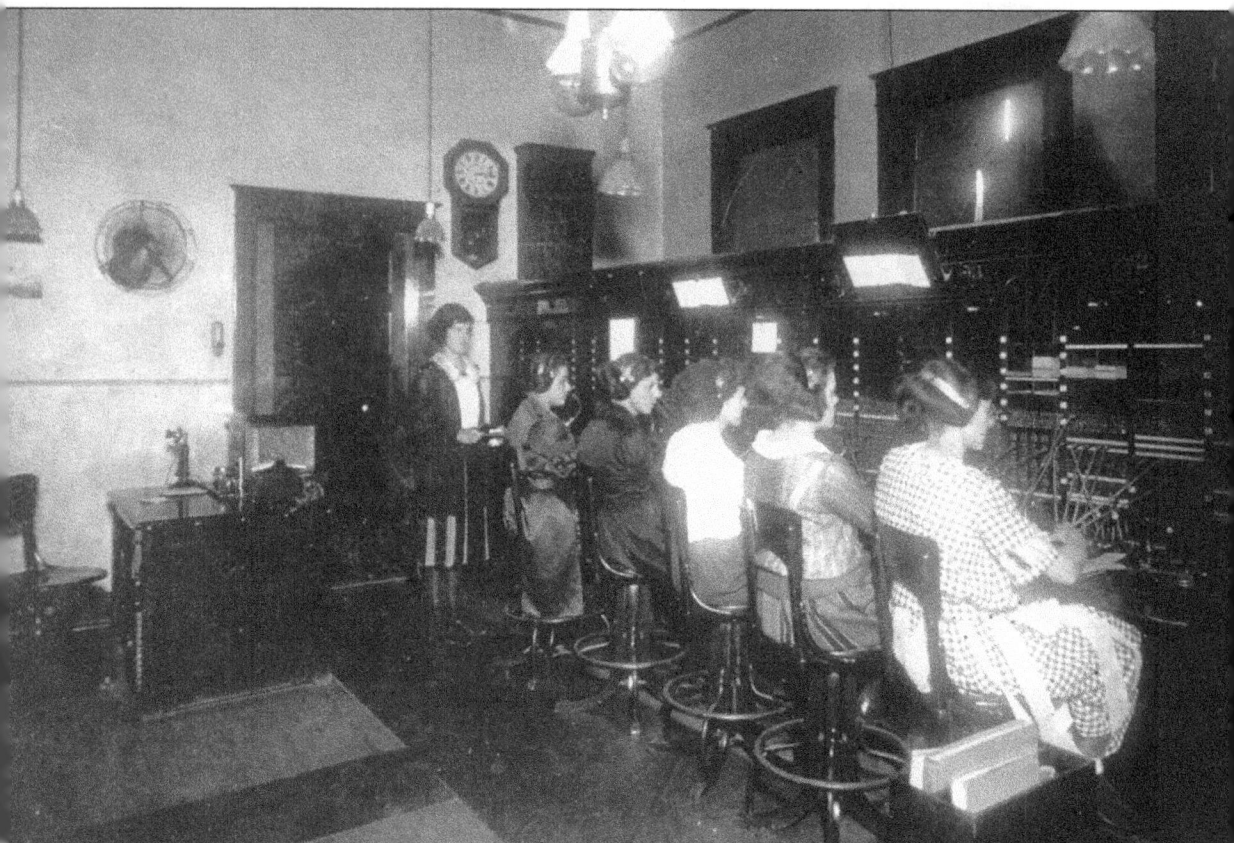

The Morris telephone switchboard and its operators are pictured here around 1919. Telephone calls were once routed through manual switchboards. The operator unplugged the cable from the incoming line and plugged it into the line for the person or party line that the caller wanted to reach.

This is the Stevens County Hospital. A few years after Dr. C. E. Caine had converted his residence on West Seventh Street to become the Morris Hospital, the former E. J. Jones residence on West Eighth Street was equipped to become the Stevens County Hospital. Incorporators for the new hospital were Dr. E. T. Fitzgerald, Dr. J. F. Cumming, and Dr. M. L. Ransom. Dr. A. I. Arneson became affiliated with the hospital when he moved to Morris the same year (1932). Anna Enge was hired as the superintendent. The hospital had room for 18 patients. The first patient, a four-year-old boy who had broken his leg when he fell from the haymow on his father's farm, was admitted on August 10, 1932.

This hospital was located on Pacific Avenue at West Fifth Street. Dr. E. T. Fitzgerald purchased the Charles Dushek residence on Pacific Avenue in 1914 and converted it to a hospital. The home was already equipped with a modern heating plant, sewer, water, and electric lights. Very little had to be done to get it ready, except to equip it for use as a hospital. The house was originally built by John Good as his residence.

Four

CHURCHES

Faith has played an important part in the lives of Stevens County residents since its inception. Families and friends migrated together, and many times the family bible was the only book they brought with them. Many of these family bibles have found their way to the collection of the Stevens County Historical Society, and these images are a small sample of the many churches founded here. Pictured here is the Scandia Lutheran Free Church, the first church and cemetery in Stevens County, organized in 1869. At a congregational meeting in December 1879, it was decided to build a church. Although not yet completed, the church was first used in 1882.

Pictured is the Kongsvinger Lutheran Church, around 1910. Founded in 1876 by 28 Norwegians and one Swede, this church was named after the part of Norway most had emigrated from. Rev. C. Saugstad was the first pastor called, and the church met in the Krogen home, Donnelly Village School, and finally at the church built in the southwest corner of section 7 in Rendsville Township. The members of this church still meet to worship each week, and services have been in English since the Norwegian language services were phased out beginning about 1930.

Pictured here is the First Methodist Episcopal Church in 1910. The First Methodist Episcopal Church of Morris was organized in 1877 with about 14 members. The group met in homes and in Good's Hall until 1880, when a church was built on the corner of West Eighth Street and Nevada Avenue. This was replaced by a brick structure. This structure served as the Federated Church from 1940 to 1972.

Pictured is the Norwegian Evangelical Lutheran Church in Morris in 1892. This church was organized in 1877 but did not have its own building until 1896. Members voted to build a church on the lot at the corner of East Fifth Street and California Avenue, purchased earlier by the Ladies Aid. The new frame structure was erected at a cost of $2,500.

Pictured is the First Congregational Church of Christ around 1915. This church was the first organized in the village of Morris when Rev. J. L. Fonda and his wife arrived in 1873. The congregation met at the depot and school, and larger meetings were held at Good's Hall. This church was built in 1879 on the northwest corner of Sixth Street and Nevada Avenue.

Pictured here is the Assumption Church in Morris. The first Catholic services were held in the Morris railroad section house in 1870 whenever Fathers Hurley and McDermott could make it up from St. Paul. In 1876, Fr. Patrick Walsh moved to Morris, and his parish included congregations in Stevens, Pope, Traverse, Wilkin, Big Stone, and Swift Counties. This church was built in 1877 with funds donated by non-Catholic churches and area residents on land donated by the railroad. In 1878, the first Stevens County church bell was hung in the belfry and welcomed parishioners for worship. It was built during the pastorate of Rev. Charles Wensieki and served the congregation until a new, brick-veneered church was built in 1892.

Pictured is the St. Mary's Convent (Samuel Larson Home). Assumption Parish acquired a half block of property and a home, the former Samuel Larson residence, in 1910 to be used for the Sisters of St. Joseph, who opened a parochial school in the spacious church basement in 1911.

Pictured here is the Assumption Church around 1910. The building pictured was constructed under the leadership of the pastor Rev. Edward Jones and made of Kasota stone and pressed brick for the cost of $40,000. This church was built in 1906 after the one built in 1892 was completely destroyed by fire.

Pictured here is the First Lutheran Church in Morris in 1926. As the membership grew and students from the West Central School of Agriculture made this their "church home away from home," the congregation voted to build a larger church. The church property was extended to the east. A brick church building was erected by the Hancock Ness Company at a cost of approximately $20,000.

Seen here is the Zion Lutheran Church in Horton Township. Zion Lutheran Church was organized in 1896 by 12 families and built on a 40-acre plot of land in Horton Township. It was in use until 1925, when it was demolished and a new church was built. The pastor's duties included farming the land. Women sat on the left side of the church and men on the right.

Seen here is the Reque Church of Scott Township in 1903. This is the interior of the church that was destroyed by the windstorm of 1905.

St. Mary's Catholic Church in Chokio was organized during the 1890s, with the church building finished by 1897. Before that, Catholic families had services in private homes. The first church burned to the ground within a year. A new church was built and used until June 21, 1959, when the current building was dedicated.

The interior of the First Congregational Church of Morris is shown here around 1895.

This is an interior view of Assumption Church in Morris and the large ornately carved and gilded high altar, around 1910.

The Reque Church of Scott Township was named after its first pastor, Rev. Peder S. Reque. Services were conducted in homes and businesses prior to the first building, constructed in 1892. Reque Church has been housed in three church buildings. The first was struck by lightning and burned in 1898. The second was destroyed by a windstorm. The third building (pictured) was constructed in 1903. In 1939, the church steeple was removed after it was damaged in a windstorm.

Five

EARLY SETTLERS AND HOMES

This picture is said to be a log cabin from Gager's Station. Gager's Station was on Wintermute Lake and a stop on the Wadsworth Trail that was used to transport supplies from St. Cloud to Fort Wadsworth (Sisseton) in Dakota Territory. Horse thieves and a whisky barrel were said to greet visitors there. This photograph was taken in the 1930s.

Gen. Theodore Barrett was best known in Stevens County as the owner of a large farm, the Barrett Ranch, which sprawled over 16,120 acres (1898) in Donnelly, Eldorado, and Rendsville Townships and into Grant County. Born in New York in 1834, he came to western Minnesota as a surveyor, bought land here, and made this his home. The ranch was the site of a large mansion of about 20 rooms and featured a tower where General Barrett could watch the ranch activity. He died as the result of a fall from his horse. General Barrett fought in the last battle of the Civil War at Palmetto Ranch in Texas, a battle fought after the war was over due to poor communication.

The Old Settler's Association was founded in 1870 to celebrate and share memories of the pioneers who came to the Stevens County area. Anyone who had settled in Stevens County as early as 1876 could become a member. According to newspaper accounts, the day and the drive to the Barrett Ranch House at Moose Island were delightful. At least 200 people were present at this Old Settler's Picnic. A bountiful repast was spread, after which the meeting was called to order by Pres. John D. Good. This meeting in June 1892 shows the impressive Barrett mansion. General Barrett was said to climb to the top of his tower and use his Civil War spyglass to watch over his many laborers.

This photograph of an annual Old Settler's Picnic is from the late 1880s. It is said to have been held at the Wintermute Farm in Morris Township, and attendees were entertained by pioneer tales as well as the Silver Cornet Band. Charles Wintermute was one of the soldiers in 1862 that captured the 300 Dakota Indians and took them to Mankato for trial. His farm had a lake frontage of two and a half miles and a tree grove of 80 acres. He was one of the original members of the Old Settler's Association.

These former Wadsworth Trail soldiers gathered for a reunion in the 1890s. These soldiers are unidentified except for Thomas Thomasson, who is standing in the second row first on the left; Cory (from Wheaton) standing in the third row, second from left; and Henry Graham in the third row, third from left. These men were responsible for guarding teamsters and their freight on the Wadsworth Trail. The Wadsworth Trail was used by teamsters beginning in 1864 to

supply Fort Wadsworth in Dakota Territory. The trail began in St. Cloud and passed through Stearns, Pope, Stevens, Big Stone, and Traverse Counties in Minnesota before it reached the Dakota Territory. Between 1864 and 1876, thousands of pounds of freight and thousands of people traveled through Stevens County to the fort, which became known as Fort Sisseton in 1876 after the Sisseton-Wahpeton reservation it guarded.

Here is a photograph of Mary Ann Ware (wife of William Penn) with handwork from 1896. A close look at the details in this photograph shows that Ware was still doing needlework at the age of 91. Notes on the back of this photograph state she was born in Philadelphia in 1805. She migrated to Barry, Illinois, where two of her children were born and then to Morris in 1880.

This photograph, captured in 1874, was taken of the Ole Larson Jesness family the year before they came to Stevens County by oxcart and settled in Swan Lake Township.

Heman W. Stone came to Morris in 1876 from southern Minnesota (Belle Plaine and LeSueur), where he had been in the milling business. In 1878, he purchased land near the Pomme de Terre River, just east of Morris, and built the Riverside Mill. He also engaged in farming and introduced red polled Hereford cattle into Stevens County. For a time he served in the state legislature. He was married to Polly Wells, a sister of H. H. Wells, a pioneer merchant in Morris. The lady in center front is Mrs. Stone's mother, Hannah Cass Wells. Mr. and Mrs. Stone were the parents of A. A. Stone; Mary (Stone) Hagerman, wife of O. S. Hagerman; Ida (Stone) Munro, wife of W. J. Munro; Eudora (Stone) Randall, wife of W. W. Randall; Royal Stone; and H. W. Stone Jr., who are pictured with their spouses and children in 1894.

Thomas Thomasson was one of the earliest settlers in Stevens County. A lieutenant in Company H, the first regiment of the state militia organized in the area, Thomasson and his family were among the first settlers in Scandia Township (later Framnas). He was the first postmaster of the Scandia Post Office in 1867 and, in 1881, traveled from St. Cloud to Morris bearing the linen plat map currently in the collection of the Stevens County Historical Society and Museum. Seen here are, from left to right, (first row) Josephine Matilda, Thomas (father), Tilda "Tillie" Jannett, Georgine (mother), and Louise Johannah; (second row) Hegbert, Thorvald, Inger Marie, Lawrence, and Hilfred. This photograph is from the 1890s.

William Wunsch was one of the pioneer settlers of Morris, walking here from Benson on July 4, 1870. He purchased land in Morris Township and lived there until 1876. At that time he bought a saloon in Morris and conducted that business on the east side of Atlantic Avenue until his retirement. The home was erected on Montana Avenue, near the courthouse.

Wunsch, pioneer settler and prominent businessman, is pictured driving near his home on Montana Avenue. Before building this home, the Wunsch family lived in the Chimneys, the beautiful home on Park Avenue purchased from the Stantons.

This Morris home on Park Avenue was built in 1880 by Lewis H. Stanton, son of President Lincoln's secretary of war. This house is affectionately known today as the Chimneys and previously as Stanton's Folly.

This was the Barrett Ranch house after extensive remodeling. Older adults of the area often told of exploring this abandoned home in the 1930s. One of their more memorable moments from these experiences was seeing the massive law books that were still on the library shelves. These books were once owned by General Barrett. Eventually sections of this structure were moved to other locations and used in various ways.

Edwin J. Jones, who came to Stevens County in 1878, was a lumber merchant in Morris and also owned yards in several surrounding towns. He later served several terms as a state senator. Jones served as the first mayor of Morris when the city charter was adopted. He developed the Crocus Valley Farm, which later became part of the West Central School of Agriculture. The home pictured here was built in 1900 on West Eighth Street. Note the huge porch that swept around the side of the home. A decorator from Minneapolis, George Hogan, was hired to do the interior. He liked the town so well he decided to move here and was in great demand to decorate both commercial and residential properties.

William Zahl was a prominent farmer in Swan Lake Township, having homesteaded there in the 1870s. His home, shown here, was located on the east shore of Pomme de Terre Lake. It had two bedrooms on the first floor and seven on the second floor to accommodate the large family. The 13-room house burned in 1965. The original portion of the house was built in 1880.

William Gausman was one of the early settlers of Pepperton Township. He was married to Hulda Drechsler in 1887, and the couple farmed until retirement in 1923. Gausman served as a county commissioner, was a member of the board of directors of the Stevens County Agricultural Society and a member of the District No. 25 school board. He died in 1939 at age 81. This picture was taken in 1910.

Pictured are the Herman Asmus family and farmhouse in Everglade Township. From left to right are Louise, Erma, Bertha (mother), Olga, Herman (father), Ed, and Walter. Wicker carriages were being manufactured in the United States by the 1880s. By the 1890s, carriages had footrests and reclining backs. A child could lie down and sleep, so it was called a "go-cart sleeper."

Six

EDUCATION

The early pioneers of Stevens County believed in education. Their aspirations made possible the schools of today and the 71 districts organized in those in-between years. Hampered by poor transportation and roads, districts were built within walking distance for and by the families of each township. This map page illustrates the locations of all 71 Stevens County school districts. The largest numbers relate to the actual school district.

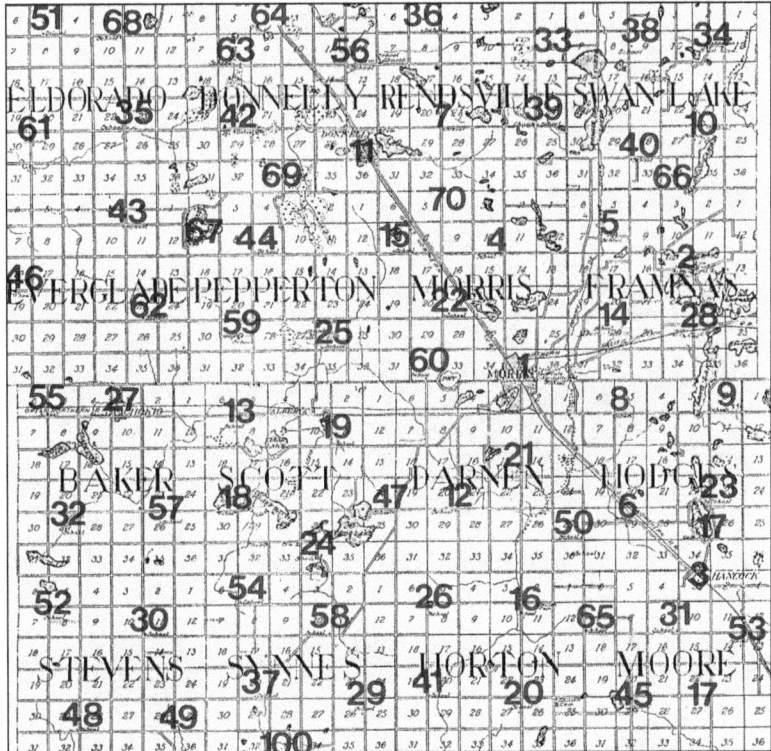

This is the Central School in Morris. The building was built in 1872 as the Stevens County Courthouse and was later used as a school. It was located on the northeast corner of Oregon Avenue and East Fifth Street.

This is a picture of school district No. 19's Farwell School around 1894. Rural schools were often referred to by a nearby farm family name rather than a district number, hence the name Farwell School. This building was moved into Alberta in 1912 and was remodeled as a dwelling for the first principal of the Alberta Consolidated School, Fred Grafelman. Seen here are, from left to right, (first row) photographer's wife and child, Elizabeth Foley, Rose Busse, Florence Hardin, Frances Busse, Rebecca Farwell, Joe Horrigan (holding slate), Mark Farwell, Ferris Hardin, Merle Farwell, Daniel Horrigan, and William Horrigan; (second row) Nora Hardin, Nina Farwell, Helen Darrow, Mrs. Nelson Darrow, Maud Darrow, Bert Horrigan, George Busse, Timothy Vaughn, Edward Horrigan, Ezra Hardin, Felix Busse, Luke Foley, James Foley, Mason Darrow, Patrick Vaughn, John Horrigan, Ray Roberts, and R. H. Grace (teacher).

The wind blew whatever paint was ever put on this building right off. School district No. 17 was formally organized on March 18, 1879. It was located in Moore Township on the northeast corner of section 27. The date of this photograph is estimated to be between 1880 and 1908. Seen here are, from left to right, (first row) Sylvester McCarthy, ? Sweeny, John Terrill, Emil Mecklenburg, Herman Mecklenburg, Henry McCarthy, Arthur Biesterfeld, Martin Biesterfeld, ? Sweeny, Elsie Mecklenburg, Lena Osterman, Louise Mecklenburg, Ina Terrill, and Alma Senholtz; (second row) John Suhrbier, John Osterman, John Mecklenburg, August Osterman, Vernus Suhrbeir, Albert Terrill, Willie Osterman, Mary Osterman, Alma Biesterfeld, Frieda Mecklenburg, and Miss Keating, the teacher.

Pictured here is school district No. 4 in 1910. On March 29, 1873, M. L. Torpey and others petitioned the county school board for permission to open this school. It was built on the northeast corner of section 15 in Morris Township shortly thereafter.

This is school district No. 20 pictured sometime between 1905 and 1910. Organized in 1884, Homer Eddy and James Milan both served as clerks. After consolidation, the building became the township government meeting hall. Seen here are, from left to right, (first row) Walter Schieve, Edward Schieve, Gustave Schlueter, Christ Schieve, Adolph Mumm, William Mumm, Charles Wille, August Mesenbrink, Martha Schlueter, Emma Mesenbrink, Clara Wille, Emma Schlueter, Martha Mesenbrink, and Louise Wille; (second row) Edwin Mumm, Leonard Schlueter, Henry Wille, Ernest Mesenbrink, Ted Schieve, Ed Mesenbrink, Emma Wille, and Lillian Ortman, the teacher.

School district No. 59 was organized in 1899 and located in the southwest corner of section 26 of Pepperton Township. The building is pictured around 1930.

School district No. 14 was originally located in the southeast corner of section 19 on the A. C. Satter farm. From 1878 until 1908, when Framnas Township residents decided it needed to be more centrally located, children walked to and from the school there. In 1908, the school was relocated to section 29 on land purchased from Andria Olson. Then the school was moved once again in 1935. The Works Progress Administration, founded by Pres. Franklin Roosevelt, built both this schoolhouse and the District No. 33 schoolhouse. Both were constructed from fieldstone gathered and split by local out-of-work residents. They had full basements and windowsills made with granite from the Ortonville quarry. After the school closed and students were bused to town, it became a school for the mentally challenged, and then the Jehovah's Witness Kingdom Hall. In 2005, it became the home for Morning Sky Greenery, a firm specializing in native prairie plants.

Shown here is the Alberta School and teachers manse in 1917. This school was built after much controversy in the village of Alberta, home to school district No. 19. Pepperton Township's District No. 25 had been the home to the school where Alberta residents sent their children for the first year, as they had not built their school yet. The walk was up to two and a half miles long, usually cold or wet, and much talk about the ruining of patent leather was bandied about. The school consolidation law of 1911 was used to force the closure of District No. 25, and this school was built in 1912. The manse, a modern home for teachers, was built in 1916.

The Rockefeller Foundation donated $4,000 to the Alberta School to build a complete modern home for teachers. This was a new concept and was written up in the *National Review*, *The Farmer*, and many other publications. It was decided that a model of the school and manse be sent to the world's fair in San Francisco in 1917. Mrs. Fred Grafelman, the superintendent's wife, created the model, including all the trees and animals.

In 1931, a fire destroyed the school and all its records. A new school was built, but in the 1950s, Alberta, Chokio, and a number of small rural districts consolidated. The elementary and junior high children traveled to Chokio and the high school students to Alberta. Pictured is the Alberta School after the 1931 fire.

This is the Alberta High School home economics class in 1917. The home economics classroom was located on the lower level of the manse, the home built for teachers with funds granted by the Rockefeller Foundation. The lower level also housed a sewing room, model dining room, laundry room, and toilet room. The superintendent and family had an apartment on the main floor, and lady teachers had rooms on the upper level.

Shown here are Alberta's consolidated school buses in 1917. After the consolidation of District Nos. 19 and 25, some children had to travel six to seven miles each way to school. During the winter, horse-drawn school buses on sleigh runners carried them to and from school. In 1913, when District No. 13 joined, they too were bused to Alberta.

These are the Hancock school buildings in 1912. This photograph was taken shortly after the 1912 completion of the new Hancock High School.

This is the Lincoln School on the east side of Morris. This building occupied the site of the present Stevens Community Medical Center. It was used until 1914, when the new high school was built on East Sixth Street. It was on the far edge of town in its day.

The Longfellow School was located on block 19, "Original Town." It was built in 1885 with an addition made in 1894 and was used as a high school and grammar school. It was demolished in 1934 and replaced with a new building, also known as Longfellow School. Other buildings that used the same site were a small frame building built in 1873 and a four-room frame building that was built in 1880 but burned in 1884.

Shown here is the Longfellow School building in 1935. The building is now used for residential apartments and offices.

Located on the corner of Sixth Street and Columbia Avenue, the original Morris High School building was built in 1914. The addition of the gymnasium and its stage expanded the programs of the Morris High School. When a new high school was built in 1968, the building became the home of the Morris Elementary School. It was used until the fall of 2005 when the new elementary school was built next to the Morris High School.

Pictured above is the boarding school for American Indians founded by the Sisters of Mercy in 1888. It became the Morris Industrial School for Indians, a federally operated boarding school, in 1892. In 1910, the school site was transferred to the state of Minnesota and became the West Central School of Agriculture. Finally the University of Minnesota, Morris campus was established on the same location in 1960.

Seven

FAMILY LIFE AND LEISURE

Before the days of the modern funeral home, it was common practice to keep the casket carrying the deceased at the family home until the funeral. It was also a common practice to conduct the funeral at the family home. Flowers were sent to the home and displayed there along with a portrait of the deceased. Portrayed here is the casket of Samuel Larson, pioneer Stevens County businessman.

Members of the Rollin Hall family of Morris Township are shown here out for a tour of Stevens County with a horse and buggy and bicycle on July 7, 1901.

Veterinarian George E. Maughan of rural Morris and his family are pictured here at the "Big Slough." Dr. Maughan came to Stevens County in 1879. Seen in this picture are George E. Maughan (the man with gun); Robert Colyer and an unidentified person (in the back seat of buggy); and Martha Louise (Colyer) Maughan, wife of George E. Maughan, and daughters Louise and Kathryn (in front seat of buggy).

Thomas and Georgine Thomasson listen to their youngest child, Tilda Jannett, age 14, playing the piano in their Morris home. This photograph was taken on a Sunday afternoon in 1899 and sent to their son Hilfred Thomasson, who was serving in Manila, the capital of the Philippines, during the Spanish American War.

An unknown group of women and children are shown wading across a stream near Hancock. The photograph was taken around 1900.

Three Hancock women at leisure read by bicycles near a tent in 1895.

The Brisbane family delights in skating near the Walter Brisbane farm in 1913. Seen here are, from left to right, Beatrice Brisbane (daughter of Aldis and Bessie Brisbane) and Lester and Gladys Brisbane (children of Walter Brisbane). Walter Brisbane farmed in section 10 of Framnas Township in Stevens County.

Prairie chickens were numerous in pioneer days and were the main course at many home and church suppers, as well as providing sport for visitors. Early train crews even stopped the train to shoot a few chickens. Bags of 50 to 100 were common. The Dakota Native Americans who lived, traveled, and buried their dead throughout Stevens County before and after the settlers came, knew the area that became Morris as "the place where they hang the chickens."

This image of hunters and their dog was captured on Jack O'Brien's farm. The O'Brien family came to Stevens County in 1879 and settled on a farm in Stevens Township. Jack O'Brien and his brother moved to Morris in 1920. O'Brien owned a big Ford trimotor plane and was killed when the plane crashed in 1933.

Shown here is the Morris Coal Trestle in 1910. These Morris High School students are shown climbing the Morris Coal Trestle. They were looking for a bird's-eye view of the Morris skyline. The adventurous young women in the white dresses are rather daring for their era.

Here is another image of the Morris Coal Trestle from 1910. These unidentified Morris High School students have reached the top of their world in this photograph.

The above hunters with their pheasants are pictured in the 1930s. Pheasant hunting is still a popular sport in Stevens County. Several farmers even raise pheasants to supplement their farming income. Below is an image of Stevens County trappers with skins and rifles.

The Grand Army of the Republic (GAR) held its semiannual encampment at Morris on June 12–15 in 1888. Visitors arrived from all parts of Minnesota. The encampment site was what is now West Seventh Street and Wyoming Avenue. On opening day, the old soldiers marched to the depot to meet Gov. Andrew McGill, who later addressed the crowd. The mammoth tent erected for the encampment blew down in a fierce storm the second night. The grand parade on Thursday was called "the grandest procession ever seen on the streets of Morris." A sham battle was held that evening where invading forces attacked the defenders of the island in Crystal Lake. The visitors disbanded and left for their homes on July 15.

This is the Decoration Day parade on East Fifth Street in 1888 in Morris. The GAR members decorated the graves. A program was held in the courthouse with speakers and music, including a male quartet accompanied by an orchestra.

Children are seen here assembled on the boardwalk for Decoration Day in the 1890s. Activities in Morris included the Overton Post marching to the cemetery to decorate the graves and a patriotic program at the Indian Industrial School.

This photograph shows Red Cross volunteers on parade around 1918. Lois Caine, the daughter of Dr. C. E. Caine, is one of the women holding a corner of the parade flag. Donors tossed contributions to the Liberty Loan Program into the flag to support the war effort.

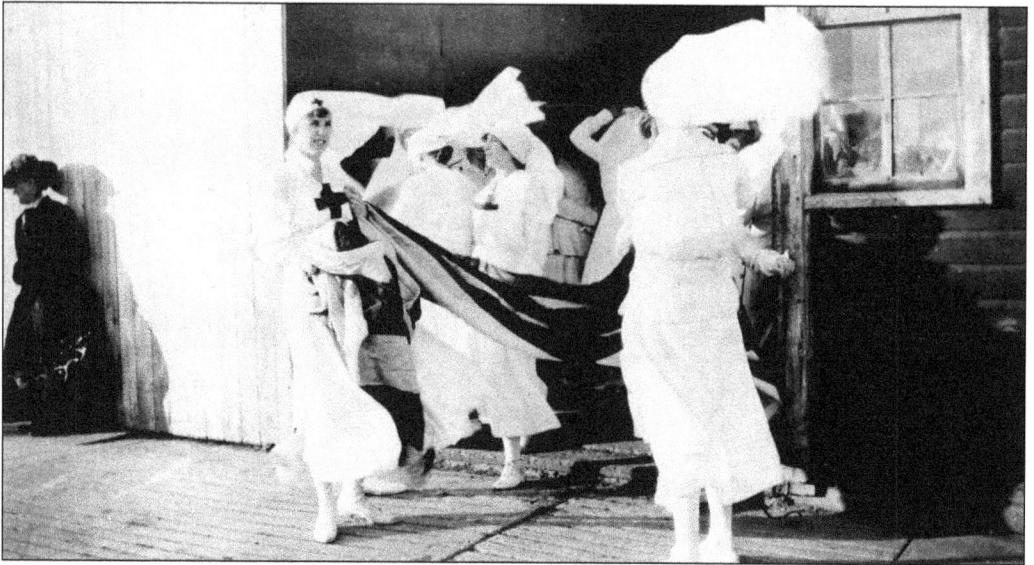

Here is another photograph of Red Cross volunteers from 1918. The Red Cross was a vital philanthropic institution, especially as it provided medical care to wounded soldiers during World War I.

Pictured here are World War I soldiers in 1918. This is a photograph of the parade of the first soldiers who left Morris for training camp during World War I. Businesses in the background are, from left to right, Stewart's Mill, Stewart's Mill office, Max Trantow's saloon, the Stevens County Creamery, and Walker Towle (dry goods).

Here is the Morris Band marching in a parade on Atlantic Avenue as Morris residents look on with civic pride.

A crowd awaiting the Spanish American War troop train is photographed in 1898.

Welcome home! George Darling and other family members welcome Earl, Robert, and Harry Darling home from the war in February 1919. Pictured from left to right are George Darling (father), Ed, Earl, Robert, Harry, Will, and Bill (Will's son) with gun.

This is the Morris girls basketball team. During this era, Morris girls interested in playing basketball formed a girls' Basket Ball (sic) Society and chose the coach and manager, generally from the facility staff. These girls paid 50¢ toward the benefit of the girls' athletics. The number of games and practices were subject to the weather. Other teams did not necessarily play in the same style as the Morris athletes, resulting in occasional controversy. The traveling team was hosted by the home team, with supper and entertainment before the return home the next day. Pictured from left to right are Bertha Watzke, Rebecca Flynn, Mildred Ortman, Charlotte Borrill, and Irene Flutner.

This is a photograph of the 1909 Morris High School football team. Uniforms were not needed in the first days of high school football in Stevens County. This photograph was hand numbered for identification: 1. Archie Stone, 2. Olaf Satter, 3. Alfred Cairney, 4. Hjalmar Dohlen, 5. Edwin Nelson, 6. Robert Darling, 7. Ben Treischel, 8. Dick Anderson, 9. Jack McDonald 10. Boyd Borrill, and 11. Cyrus Ortman.

Pictured here is the 1914 Morris High School basketball team. These players, unidentified except for Archie Stone (third from right) and Jack Ortman (fourth from right), did not play in uniforms.

This is the Alberta Baseball Club of 1914. Seen here, from left to right, are George Ginnow (mascot), George Gieb, Mark Farwell, Ben Loher, John Luhman, John Schultz (manager), John Grossman, Albert Wilson, Gene Wilson, and Dean Jackson.

This is the 1910 Hancock baseball team. Until the later 1900s, managers did not wear uniforms, opting instead for a formal suit and tie.

Sulky races were a highly enjoyable pastime. Fast horses were a source of considerable pride to their owners. This photograph, looking north from Fifth Street, was taken in about 1910. A close inspection shows cement sidewalks, electric power poles, and automobiles.

This is a picture of a racehorse called Bangum from around 1910. The horse was owned by William Wunsch, a prominent Stevens County resident and saloon owner.

Eight

MAIN STREET

This building was the second Stevens County Courthouse. The first courthouse was built in 1872 in the block now occupied by the public library. The second courthouse was erected in 1883 at a cost of $17,500. Stone from the surrounding prairie was used for the foundation, and much of the brick used was of local manufacture. In its early days, it was more than a courthouse. The courtroom featured raised seats and a stage where many entertainments, political rallies, and community gatherings were held. The present courthouse was built directly in front of this building in the late 1950s, and the old structure was demolished.

Pictured is Main Street in Alberta in 1913. The Mitlyng Building is on the left; Foley's Hall is the white building with awning. The elevators are, from left to right, Lang Elevator, Winter Elevator, and Eames Elevator.

Pictured here is Chokio's Main Street in 1908. Power lines, horses, automobiles, and pedestrians could be found in Chokio in 1908. The stores are, from front to back, (left side of the street) a theater, Commercial Hotel, Commoner Hotel, Chokio Post Office, and a drugstore; (right side of the street) an advertisement for McDonald Brothers Show, Saturday, June 5; A. Olson Blacksmith Shop; and the Chokio Restaurant.

The top image is a bird's-eye view of Donnelly looking toward the northwest. The photograph was taken before the fire in 1916. The railroad park is on the left, and the Presbyterian church is in the center background. The bank building is on the far left with the hotel across the street. Below is another view of Donnelly.

Here is a bird's-eye view of Front Street in Hancock in 1910. The two-story building in the background is the village hall. The Ritz Café was further down the street; next was the First National Bank. The Swen Swenson residence was on the corner.

Shown here is Atlantic Avenue in Hancock, photographed in 1913. The large building on the right is the John Erickson Hardware. The Nystuen Brothers occupied one of the brick buildings in the left foreground. The tall building in the background is the village hall.

Shown here is Atlantic Avenue in Morris, pictured in 1915. The two buildings on the left are still standing today, home to several businesses.

This is a bird's-eye view of Morris looking southeast from a railroad coal chute.

Nine

TRANSPORTATION

H. J. Quigley Feed Barn at Morris is seen here on a busy day in 1905. The livery barn provided a place for farmers to leave their horses when they were in town for the day and gave them shelter, water, and hay. The livery also rented horses and carriages to out-of-town travelers, absentee landowners who came to check their properties, and to "locals" who needed conveyances for group outings.

Bell, Grace, and Harry Hall go out for a buggy ride around 1900.

This unidentified man has paused in front of the Morris Fire Hall during his winter excursion.

The Kerl and Watzke blacksmith shop is pictured in the 1890s. This blacksmith shop was on Sixth Street in Morris. The location is now the parking lot behind the City Center Mall.

Officers from the Dreveskraght Land Office wait outside their storefront in an automobile and horse and buggy. They are about to take a party of land buyers on a tour of available Stevens County properties. This photograph is from 1910.

Donnelly depot, a section crew, and gandy dancers are photographed here in 1900. Gandy dancers got their name through the use of tools made by the Gandy Manufacturing Company of Chicago. The slim man by the telephone pole was tentatively identified as John Baldy.

These men are digging the Great Northern Railroad "subway" tracks in Hancock around 1907. E. J. Stiefel worked for Great Northern Railroad as a surveyor and crew chief in the period from 1900 to 1910. Great Northern Railroad cut a new grade through Hancock in 1907 to reduce a hill that was stalling freight trains. The new cut was known locally as the "subway."

Train wrecks were a hazard of early train travel, and their aftermath was a must-see event.

Pictured here is a train engine stuck in the snow in Morris after the blizzard of 1917. The engine is stuck directly south of the Eagles Ball Park entrance.

Muddy roads and streets challenged the enthusiasm of drivers in the early days of automobile travel. As is so often the situation, more people liked to talk about the problem than do something about it.

This elevating grader, pulled by a Caterpillar and owned by Harry Day, was a great improvement over the old horse-drawn scrapers. Dirt could be elevated from the side to the roadbed, or placed in wagons or dump trucks and hauled to fill in low spots. Note the cook car/bunkhouse at the side. The cook and the machine man stayed here overnight. The cook prepared breakfast and the noon meal for the crew, and the machine man kept the machinery greased and ready for work.

Harry Day had this cook car built during the winter of 1927 to feed his road-building crews. The cook car was 10 feet by 22 feet long, the kitchen being 10 feet by 12 feet, and the bedroom being 10 feet by 10 feet. It was mounted on an old truck chassis, which had hard rubber tires.

Shown here is the bridge north of the Fred Toop farm in section 14 of Horton Township. The new bridge spanned a creek, which ran into the Pomme de Terre River. Note the boy standing on the old bridge in the background.

Following county ditching projects that began in 1906, land buyers are lined up and ready to go out and look at thousands of acres that had been underwater but were now available for farming. John Grove, a dealer in farmland, led this group of land buyers out to look at "Farms That Are Farms" on August 8, 1912. The Homestead Act of 1912 reduced the homestead occupation requirement to three years from five, so some of these buyers may have had that in mind. Grove's land office was located at the back of the bank building on the corner of Atlantic Avenue and Seventh Street in Morris. That building now houses Bremer Bank.

At a time when long-distance travel was done by passenger train, a vehicle such as this would meet travelers at the depot and bring them to the hotel on Pacific Avenue. It was the taxi of that time.

Bicycles were a reliable mode of transportation and quite sporty for the female sex. Lydia Whitcomb came to Hancock in about 1890 and was employed at the Wilcox and Wells Store. In 1895, she married Sam Pape, the Great Northern Railroad depot agent. Lydia was very active in the civic, social, and religious life of the community. She died at Hancock in 1949.

Ford Tri Motor Owne
Kenyon Transportatio
Morris, M
16 Passenger Two Piol
In Feet From Tip To

The first airplane in Stevens County, a Travel Aire, was purchased in March 1928 by Leroy "Roy" Woolridge and Jess M. Kenyon, owner of the Morris Hotel, for the price of $3,000. In November of that same year, Woolridge flew home from Wichita, Kansas, in this trimotor plane they had purchased with their partner, Russell Riggs, and with financial aid from Jack O'Brien for $28,000. Clyde Ice, of Rapid City, South Dakota, owner of the first trimotor plane in the United States, also contributed funds. The Kenyon Transportation Company was a daring

venture as neither partner was yet licensed for commercial travel and many saw air travel as just an exciting amusement. The man in the white cap, under the middle propellor, is Roy Woolridge. To his right is Charles Lindbergh and to his left is Amelia Earhart, who was given flying lessons by Woolridge. Of Earhart, Woolridge was often heard to say, "I didn't think she'd ever learn to fly."

Fred Pasche stands with his plane in a Stevens County field.

Fred Pasche's Curtis J. N. 4-C airplane crash, in the fall of 1929, is shown here.

Ten

WEATHER

A tar paper shanty is nearly covered by snow on the Anton Johnson farm after the blizzard of 1909.

Mrs. F. H. Richardson is pictured in front of the Richardson home on Park Avenue in Morris. Walks were cleared by hand, using a shovel.

Chokio's Main Street is buried in snow after a blizzard in 1917. Old-timers said that winter was the worst since 1892. The photograph shows the west side of Main Street with the G. S. Lines Merchandise store, which later became the Virnig store, at the left. The large building to the north is the McNally building.

Pictured here is the weather station at the West Central School of Agriculture. The photograph is from around 1912.

Stone's Mill Dam on the Pomme de Terre River is shown in this photograph. This picture, looking east at the foot of the sluiceway, was taken in April 1897 shortly after the dam broke. The bank on the opposite side has a snow drift about 18 feet deep.

Chokio children are pictured here frolicking in floodwaters. The Chokio School is the large building in background.

This flooded street scene was captured in Morris in front of the J. J. Geib Lumber Company on June 14, 1914. The lumber company was located at 817 Atlantic Avenue.

This is an image of a flood on the Pomme de Terre River. The photograph was taken looking east on March 28, 1905. The Charles Johnson Bridge can be seen in the center. Trees show the original riverbed.

CYCLONE AT HANCOCK MINN · AUG. 15 ·1914.

Here is a photograph of the aftermath of the cyclone that hit Hancock on August 15, 1914. This storm was considered to be one of the worst windstorms ever experienced in this area. Much damage occurred in Rendsville and Moore Townships, where a number of barns and granaries were destroyed, and grain, stored in shocks and stacks, was blown about. The tragic death of Moses Durkee occurred in the Hancock area. He was riding on a hayrack when he was overtaken by the storm. The wind lifted the rack from the wagon and demolished it, which resulted in Durkee's death.

Visit us at
arcadiapublishing.com

www.ingramcontent.com/pod-product-compliance
Lightning Source LLC
Chambersburg PA
CBHW050558110426
42813CB00008B/2396